MW01681178

This book is dedicated to the memory
of my beloved parents.

Your love, wisdom, and strength remain with me always,
guiding my steps and inspiring all that I am.

BMR

DIVINE HOUSE
BOOKS

ISBN: 979-889589284-8

SURVIVING GRIEF'S SILENT ARRIVAL

REFLECTIVE JOURNEY OF HEALING AND HOPE

Dwantrina Russell

Contents

Introduction

There is a unique sound that a heart makes when it shatters—silent to the world but deafening to the soul. During grief, it's easy to feel like those pieces are lost forever, scattered like dust in the wind. But as I sat with the remnants of my broken heart, something unexpected happened. I began to see them not as pieces of what once was but as the building blocks of something new.

Grief has a way of making you feel as if everything is falling apart, and the life you once knew has crumbled into countless fragments. But what if those aren't just broken pieces to be discarded? What if they're part of a divine design, waiting to be reassembled into something even more beautiful?

The pieces of my life, though jagged and scattered, were each essential. Together, they formed a mosaic—a beautiful tapestry of experiences, emotions, and memories that, when put together, created something entirely new. The process was not easy, and the journey was not without pain, but in the breaking, there was a blessing. And to find true peace, I needed to embrace every part of my journey. The joy and the sorrow, the triumphs, and the tears—each played a vital role, adding meaning to the larger story of my life. And as I began to fit these pieces together, I discovered that my breakdown was not a sign of defeat, but of strength.

This book is my story—one of finding peace in every piece. It's a testament to the power of grace during grief, and the beauty that can emerge from the broken places in our lives. As you journey through these pages, may you find the courage to embrace your brokenness, trusting that every fragment is part of a greater purpose. And in doing so, may you find the peace that surpasses all understanding, as you are gently restored, piece by piece.

Chapter 1:
The Uninvited Guest

The day started like any other—a fresh morning, a quiet prayer, and the sun rising with a promise. I remember feeling a sense of peace, a little hope, thinking that maybe the day would bring some kind of breakthrough. The routine felt comforting, familiar. But then, the phone rang.

You know, it's strange how a single sound can change everything. One moment, you're in the middle of something simple, and the next, your entire world shifts. I picked up the phone, not expecting anything out of the ordinary. But the voice on the other end—the words they spoke— hit me with the force a ton of bricks. It was the kind of news that stops time.

I stood there, frozen, with the phone in my hand, as the room around me seemed to fade. The world, which just moments ago had felt full of life, went eerily quiet. My heart pounded, my hands trembled I wanted to move, to speak, to do something—but I couldn't. I found myself trapped in that painful in-between, torn between the life I once knew and the new reality that had just come crashing down.

Grief entered my life at that moment. Not with a warning or a gentle nudge, but with a brutal force that left me gasping for air. It didn't knock or ask for permission; it barged in, uninvited, and refused to leave. The day, once so ordinary, was now painted with a heavy, suffocating weight. Grief settled into my chest heavy as a stone, changing everything—the way I moved, the way I breathed, the way I felt.

I somehow made it through the day, though I can barely remember how. It was a blur of numbness, of going through the motions without really being present. My body was there, but my heart and mind were elsewhere trying to make sense of the unimaginable. That night, I crawled into bed, hoping that sleep might offer some kind of escape, but even rest wouldn't come easily. Grief was too loud, too persistent. Every time I closed my eyes, it was there, pulling me deeper into the pain.

By the next morning, the world outside looked the same, but I didn't. The sun rose, and people carried as though it was just another day. But for me, nothing was the same. Reality had set in. I wasn't waking up from some bad dream. This was my new life, and grief was right there with me, already woven into every part of it.

I didn't know what to do with it. Grief had no face, no form, yet it was everywhere—It didn't scream or shout; it just quietly tapped me on the shoulder, reminding me that it was there, and it wasn't going anywhere. The life I had known before felt as if it had crumbled, and I was left standing in the wreckage, unsure of how to move forward.

Days turned into weeks, and it became clear that grief was not a temporary visitor. It had taken up permanent residence in my life. No amount of wishing, crying, or pretending could make it leave. It was there in the quiet moments, lurking in the corners of my mind, an uninvited guest who refused to leave. Grief didn't need permission to enter, and once it was there, it consumed every part of my being. It didn't just sit in the background—it was always ready to spring forth with full force at the slightest provocation.

I'd hear a song we used to listen to, catch a whiff of their favorite fragrance, or see a place we used to visit, and the memories would overtake me, crashing into me with the force of a freight train. I couldn't escape it. Any of these could trigger its sudden return, flooding my senses with the unbearable pain of loss. A tidal wave would rise without warning, pulling me under in an instant.

One moment, I could be going about my day, holding myself together, and the next, I would be drowning in an ocean of emotions, gasping for air. Grief was relentless. There were times when I thought I could push through, that maybe I had finally turned a corner. But then, out of nowhere, it would strike again, as raw, and overwhelming as the first day I'd experienced it. It didn't care about my schedule, my responsibilities, or my attempts at moving forward. It showed up whenever it wanted, filling my mind with the weight of everything I had lost.

There were days when I would sit in silence, numb from the sheer weight of it all, feeling as though I was suspended between two worlds—the one I had known before and the one I now inhabited, where nothing felt familiar. I was a stranger in my own life, navigating the strange new terrain of grief. It was exhausting, and the heaviness of it seeped into every part of me, even on days when I thought I had finally caught my breath.

What I hadn't expected was how grief would weave itself

into the mundane moments, quietly altering the landscape of my everyday life. It wasn't just present in the big, significant memories; it was there when I opened the fridge, when I folded laundry, or when I heard the sound of laughter in another room. It clung to the simplest routines, wrapping itself around even the most ordinary tasks, making everything feel foreign and distant.

I would lie awake at night, the silence amplifying my thoughts, and grief would rise again, relentless in its pursuit. It filled the room, a shadow I couldn't escape, stretching the nights into something long and endless. The stillness was both a comfort and a curse—it was the only time I felt the weight of my loss without distraction, yet it was also when the pain seemed most unbearable.

And then there was the unpredictability of it all. There were no patterns, no warning signs to prepare me. Grief was a storm, calm one minute, violent the next, and I had no control over when it would rage or when it would subside. Some days, I could function—go through the motions, smile, even laugh—but other days, it would blindside me, dragging me into the darkness before I even knew what hit me.

I wanted to outrun it, to leave it behind, but grief doesn't work that way. It doesn't follow an easy path. It twists and turns, circles back on itself, and takes you to places you never expected to go. And as much as I tried to escape it, grief had a way of pulling me deeper into its grasp, forcing me to confront the emptiness that had been left behind.

Yet, somewhere in that labyrinth of sorrow, I began to believe that this was my new reality – So I thought. Grief had changed me, shaped me in ways I hadn't anticipated. And maybe, just maybe, that wasn't entirely a bad thing. In the breaking, in the shattered pieces, there was a strange kind of clarity. I began to see that grief was not my enemy, but a reflection of the love I had lost, the depth of my connection to the person I mourned. It was a reminder that to love deeply is to grieve deeply, and that in my pain, there was meaning.

Chapter 2:
The Stages of Grief

Grief, as I came to understand, is not a linear journey. It does not follow a predictable path or abide by a timetable. It is a chaotic, often turbulent experience that demands to be felt in all its intensity. And while we often talk about the stages of grief—denial, anger, bargaining, depression, and acceptance—there's another stage that is rarely acknowledged but crucial to the process of healing: Reclamation.

Denial

Denial was my first reaction—the disbelief that this was happening, that my world had truly been turned upside down. I wanted to cling to the hope that somehow this was all a bad dream, something I could wake up from and everything would be as it was before. But denial, as with all the stages of grief, is temporary. Reality has a way of asserting itself, no matter how much we try to resist.

Anger

Anger soon followed. It burned hot and fierce, a fire that consumed me from the inside out. I was angry at the world, at God, at myself. I raged against the unfairness of it all, the injustice of having something so precious ripped away. Anger was exhausting, but it was also energizing. It gave me something to focus on, something to channel my pain into. But it wasn't permanent. Anger is a fire that eventually burns out, leaving only ashes in its wake.

Bargaining

Bargaining was the stage where I tried to regain some control. I found myself making deals with God, with fate. "If only I do this," I would think, "maybe I can bring back what I've lost." It was a desperate attempt to turn back time, to undo the irreversible. But bargaining, much the same as denial, is a form of resistance—a refusal to accept what has happened.

Depression

Depression was the hardest stage to endure. It was a heavy, suffocating blanket that wrapped itself around me, pulling me down into a place of despair. In this stage, I felt the full weight of my loss, the emptiness that seemed to stretch on forever. Depression whispered lies into my ear, telling me that this was all there was, that I would never escape the darkness.

Acceptance

Acceptance is not a cure, and it doesn't mean that the pain goes away. Acceptance is simply the acknowledgment that what has happened cannot be changed, and that life must go on. It's the understanding that while grief is a part of you, it does not have to control you. Acceptance is the moment when you recognize that it's okay to move forward, to find a new way of being in the world.

Reclamation

Then there's the hidden stage beyond acceptance: **Reclamation**. This is the stage where you begin to reclaim your life, to rediscover who you are in the wake of your loss. It is the phase where you begin to rebuild yourself, crafting a new identity that acknowledges your grief but is not solely shaped by it.

Reclamation is the process of taking back your power, of saying, "This happened to me, but it does not have to destroy me." It's the stage where you begin to feel the stirrings of hope, where you see that there is life beyond grief. It is the stage where you rebuild, not just your life, but yourself.

Chapter 3:
Healing Through the Tough Days

Grief, with its relentless grip, seemed to have rooted itself in every part of my life. It wasn't just the sorrow that clung to me, but the heavy presence of anxiety, depression, and doubt that grew alongside it. There were days when I questioned everything, I thought I knew about faith and life. It felt as though grief was not only invading my heart but shaking the very foundations of my faith. I found myself standing at a crossroads, unsure if I had the strength to continue believing in a God who seemed to have allowed these things to happen to me.

The deep sorrow left me feeling abandoned, as though God had turned His face away during my most painful moments. My prayers, which had once flowed easily, felt hollow, empty. Sometimes, I didn't want to pray at all. What was the point of calling out to God when it seemed as though He had been silent in the midst of my suffering? Why would a loving God let me walk through such profound loss? These thoughts consumed me, and there were times when I felt completely disconnected, not only from the world but from the divine presence I had always believed in.

But even when it felt I was walking through a spiritual desert, something within me whispered that I wasn't as alone as I felt. Grief was ever-present, yes—but so was God. Even in times when I didn't have the words, the simple act of sitting in silence, of allowing my heart to reach out to the divine, began to soothe the raw edges of my grief. It didn't always come easily. There were times when I would sit with clenched fists, unwilling to speak, too angry or too exhausted to even try. But eventually, I found myself whispering simple prayers: *"Help me, God."* That was all I could manage some days, but it was enough.

Slowly, I came to understand that prayer wasn't about having the right words or even the right attitude. It was about showing up, laying everything before God—my pain, my confusion, my anger—and trusting that He was listening. Even when I didn't feel His presence, even when it seemed my prayers were bouncing off the walls, I chose to believe that God was there, waiting for me in the silence.

Grief and the Presence of God

As much as grief had taken up residence in my life, I began to understand that God was there too. It wasn't always in the obvious ways—there were no miraculous healings or sudden changes in my circumstances. In the quiet moments, I began to feel something shift. It was subtle at first, a gentle stirring deep within my soul. God's presence wasn't loud or forceful; it was quiet and constant. Though Grief clung to me as a shadow, within that shadow, I found light.

It was God's light, shining through the cracks in my broken heart, reminding me that even in my deepest sorrow, I was not forsaken. Grief had changed the way I saw the world, but it hadn't changed the truth that God was with me. It was a paradox—how could I feel both abandoned and embraced at the same time? But as I continued to pray, I found out that grief and faith could coexist. I didn't have to choose one or the other.

God wasn't asking me to deny my pain or pretend it didn't exist. He wasn't asking for perfect faith during my brokenness. Instead, He was offering me the space to bring all of it—my doubt, my anger, my sadness—before Him, trusting that He could hold it all. In the depths of my grief, God's presence wasn't about fixing what had been shattered but about sitting with me during it. He was the steady hand that held me when I felt I was falling apart, the quiet presence that reminded me that I was not alone, even when the world felt unbearably empty.

Prayer as a Bridge

Prayer became the bridge that connected my broken heart to the divine source of all comfort. It wasn't always immediate, and it certainly wasn't always easy. But over time, I began to feel the weight of grief lessen just enough to allow a sliver of hope to enter in. There is something profoundly healing about pouring your heart out to God, about laying bare your deepest pain, your fears, and your doubts. In those moments, prayer became the language of my soul.

There were times when the prayers were nothing more than tears, silent cries that my heart lifted to heaven. And yet, even those wordless prayers were met with grace. Slowly, I began to see how God was working, I wasn't the same person I had been before, and that was okay. Grief had reshaped me, and through prayer, God was helping me rebuild—piece by piece.

I learned that prayer wasn't about asking for things to go back to the way they were, but about finding peace in the way things were now. It was about trusting that even though I couldn't see the full picture, God was holding the pieces of my life together. Prayer became the place where I could be fully myself—broken, messy, and uncertain—and still be met with love.

The Coexistence of Grief and Faith

Grief didn't disappear overnight. It was still there, but so was God. Faith wasn't about ignoring the pain or pretending that everything was okay, it was about holding onto the belief that even in my deepest sorrow, God was still good. It was about trusting that He was with me, even when I couldn't feel Him.

Prayer didn't erase the grief, but it gave me the strength to carry it. It became my refuge, the place I went when I had no more strength left. Grief was a part of my story, but so was healing. And it was through prayer that I found the courage to keep walking, even when the road was long and uncertain.

In the end, it was the power of prayer that carried me through this journey. And though I still had questions, doubt, and fear, I knew that I wasn't walking this path alone. Grief was there, and so was God. In His quiet strength, I found the courage to take one step, then another, slowly finding my way forward again.

As the months passed, I began to accept that grief would be present. I stopped fighting it and allowed myself to feel the pain, as if surrendering to the waves of sorrow rather than struggling against the current. It was a slow, agonizing process, but I started to understand that grief wasn't something to be conquered or defeated—it was there for a reason. Grief wasn't there to destroy me but to help me navigate the uncharted waters of loss. In the depths of my sorrow, grief was teaching me something—about myself, about life, about the nature of love and loss. It was revealing that in the breaking, there was a kind of beauty I had never seen before. I began to see the pieces of my shattered heart not as useless fragments scattered by the wind, but as elements of something greater. Together, they were weaving a tapestry that was both beautiful and strong, delicate yet enduring. And then, to my surprise, something amazing unfolded. It was as though I had walked out of a black-and-white world and stepped into a vibrant, colorful landscape. The darkness that had seemed so overwhelming, so suffocating, began to lift. I remember hearing Johnny Nash's song *"I Can See Clearly Now"* playing in the background, and for the first time in what seemed forever, I truly felt the lyrics resonate in my soul:

"I can see clearly now, the rain is gone.
I can see all obstacles in my way.
Gone are the dark clouds that had me blind.
It's gonna be a bright, bright sunshiny day."

The words washed over me like a summer's breeze after a long, cold storm. It was as if the rain of grief, which had poured down on me for so long, had finally passed. The clouds that had once hung low and heavy over my heart were drifting away, and in their place was a clear, boundless sky filled with light. It was refreshing—as though inhaling a deep breath after being submerged underwater for too long. The greens of renewal, the yellows of hope, the blues of peace, and the reds of passion were all flooding back into view. I realized that the shadow of grief hadn't disappeared—it had simply changed. It was no longer the looming, oppressive force that cast darkness over every aspect of my life. Instead, it had become a softer presence, a reminder of what I had lost, but also of how far I had come.

Chapter 4:
Breathe

Breathing Through the Pain

Give yourself permission to breathe. In the depths of grief, it's easy to lose sight of the present, to become so overwhelmed by pain and anxiety that you bottle everything up, hoping for the storm to pass. But taking that pause is essential. It's a reminder that you're still here, and still capable of taking the next step.

Every breath is a small victory, a quiet testament to your courage. Healing isn't about erasing the pain or ignoring its presence. It's about making room within that pain to find your strength again, to remember your purpose, and to allow yourself to feel glimpses of peace. Each moment of stillness is a step toward reclaiming your life, a step toward believing that even during sorrow, there is still beauty waiting to be found.

Grief may have changed you, but it doesn't have to define you. You are still capable of love, of laughter, and of joy.

Moving forward doesn't mean forgetting; it means honoring the past by living fully in the present. It means allowing yourself to grow, to become someone who is not defined by loss but shaped by it in ways that make you stronger, more compassionate, more alive.

So breathe deeply, and with each breath, take a step toward the life that is waiting for you. There is so much more ahead. The road may still have its challenges, but you are equipped to face them. You have the power to rise, the courage to heal, and the heart to embrace whatever comes next.

Chapter 5:
The Beauty of What Remains

So, you've made it through the murky swamp of grief, wiped away countless tears, and survived those awkward, well-meaning hugs from people who never quite knew what to say. And yet, here you are—maybe a little bruised, forever changed, but standing strong on the other side. Here's the plot twist you didn't see coming you're not just hopeful—you're free. Free from the weight that once held you down, free to embrace a life beyond what you ever thought possible. What was meant to break you has instead unlocked a door to something greater, and now you're stepping boldly into a whole new beginning. How incredible is that?

Grief has taught you that life's too precious to stay hidden inside when the storm rages. It whispers gently in those quiet moments, reminding you that healing isn't a straight path with a clear finish line. It's more like a rollercoaster, full of unexpected twists and turns. But here's the thing—you don't need to rush. You don't have to figure it all out. Just hold on, laugh when you can, and trust that you'll find your rhythm again. With every step forward, you're moving closer to a place where peace and renewal aren't just dreams—they're your reality. And your loved ones? They're not left behind. They live on in you, woven into your every smile, every laugh, and every quiet moment when you feel their presence, nudging you onward. And then there will be those moments—when joy catches you off guard, when you laugh louder than you thought possible. And you have: a new way to live, a new way to love.

Life, in all its unpredictable, messy glory, keeps moving. New experiences will unfold, new relationships will blossom, and you'll realize that your heart's capacity to love has only grown deeper. The joy you'll feel doesn't erase the grief—it's the proof that you've walked through the fire, and now you stand on the other side, fully alive.

This is your new beginning. Embrace it with all you've got.

Daily Prayers of Inspiration

Day 1: A Prayer for Strength

Heavenly Father, I come to You today seeking strength. My heart feels heavy, and the road ahead seems long and uncertain. I ask that You fill me with Your power, that I may find the strength to face each day with courage and resilience. Help me to trust in Your plan, even when I cannot see the way forward. Be my shield and my guide, and remind me that I am never alone, for You are with me always. Amen.

Day 2: A Prayer for Peace

"Peace I leave with you; my peace I give you. I do not give to you as the world gives. Do not let your hearts be troubled and do not be afraid."
— John 14:27

Lord, today I pray for peace—peace in my heart, peace in my mind, and peace in my soul. The storms of life may rage around me, but I know that Your peace surpasses all understanding. Calm the turmoil within me, and let Your peace wash over me like a gentle breeze. Help me to release my fears and anxieties into Your hands, knowing that You are in control. Fill me with Your peace, Lord, and let it guide me through this day. Amen.

Day 3: A Prayer for Hope

"May the God of hope fill you with all joy and peace as you trust in Him, so that you may overflow with hope by the power of the Holy Spirit."
— Romans 15:13

Gracious God, when the world feels dark and the future

uncertain, I ask that You fill my heart with hope. Remind me that no matter how difficult the journey may be, there is always hope in You. Help me to see the glimmers of light in the darkness, and to trust that better days are ahead. Let Your hope be the anchor for my soul, keeping me steady and secure even during trials. Thank You for the hope that You give, and for the promise of brighter tomorrows. Amen.

Day 4: A Prayer for Healing

"He heals the brokenhearted and binds up their wounds."
— Psalm 147:3

Father, I come to You in need of healing. My heart is broken, and the pain feels overwhelming at times. But I know that You are the Great Healer, and that nothing is too difficult for You. Please touch my heart and heal the wounds that grief has left behind. Restore my spirit, and bring me to a place of wholeness and peace. Help me to trust in Your timing and to be patient in the process of healing. Thank You for Your loving care, and for the healing that is already beginning in my heart. Amen.

Day 5: A Prayer for Gratitude

"Give thanks in all circumstances; for this is God's will for you in Christ Jesus."
— 1 Thessalonians 5:18

Lord, today I choose to focus on gratitude. Even in pain, I know that there are blessings all around me. Help me to see the good that still exists in my life, and to be thankful for each moment of grace. Thank You for the love of family and friends, for the beauty of creation, and for the gift of another day. May my heart be filled with gratitude, and may I share that gratitude with others, spreading Your love and light wherever I go. Amen.

Day 6: A Prayer for Guidance

"Trust in the Lord with all your heart and lean not on your own understanding; in all your ways submit to Him, and He will make your paths straight."
— Proverbs 3:5-6

Heavenly Father, I seek Your guidance today. The path ahead feels unclear, and I am unsure of which way to turn. I ask that You direct my steps and lead me in the way that I should go. Help me to trust in Your wisdom and to surrender my own understanding to You. Give me the discernment to make wise decisions and the courage to follow where You lead. Thank You for being my guide and my constant companion on this journey. Amen.

Day 7: A Prayer for Faith

"Now faith is confidence in what we hope for and assurance about what we do not see."
— Hebrews 11:1

Lord, I pray for faith—faith that moves mountains, faith that holds strong in the face of adversity, faith that trusts in Your goodness even when the world seems uncertain. Strengthen my faith, Lord, and help me to hold fast to the promises You have made. Remind me that faith is not about having all the answers, but about trusting in the One who does. May my faith be a light in the darkness, a beacon of hope and assurance that You are always with me. Amen.

Affirmations

Empowering Your Spirit: Daily Affirmations for Strength, Peace, and Divine Guidance

1. I am guided by a divine light, and every step I take leads me closer to peace and fulfillment.

2. My spirit is resilient, and I have the strength to overcome any challenge that comes my way.

3. I trust that everything unfolds according to a higher purpose, and I embrace the journey with faith.

4. In every moment, I am surrounded by love and supported by a grace greater than myself.

5. I release all fear and doubt, knowing that I am protected and provided for by the Creator.

6. Each day, I grow stronger in my faith, wiser in my actions, and more compassionate in my heart.

7. I am open to receiving the blessings that life has in store for me, and I welcome them with gratitude.

8. My challenges are opportunities for growth, and I am becoming the person I am meant to be.

9. Peace flows through me, grounding me in the present moment and guiding me toward my highest good.

10. I am a vessel of love and light, and I share that with the world around me, knowing it returns to me multiplied.

Tools for Healing

Reflect on your journey, connect with your faith, emotions, and find practical ways to move forward. Each exercise is a step toward restoration, offering you the opportunity to process your grief, reclaim your life, and embrace the hope that lies ahead.

Exercise 1: Journaling Your Journey

Purpose: *To explore and process your emotions through writing.*

1. Reflect: Set aside 10-15 minutes each day to journal about your thoughts and feelings. Write freely, without judgment. Allow yourself to express whatever is on your heart.

2. Prompt: Start with the question, "How do I feel today?" Write down whatever comes to mind, whether it's pain, hope, anger, or anything in between.

3. Reflection: After writing, take a moment to reflect on what you've written. What emotions stand out to you? What thoughts are recurring? How can you address these feelings in a healthy way?

Tip: Don't worry about grammar or structure—this is for your eyes only. The goal is to give your emotions a voice and to understand them better.

Exercise 2: Creating a Gratitude List

Purpose: *To shift focus from loss to the blessings that still exist.*

1. List: Each day, write down three things you are grateful for. These can be small—like a warm cup of tea or a kind word from a friend—or more significant, like the support of

loved ones or the strength you've found within yourself.

2. Reflect: As you write, take a moment to truly feel the gratitude for each item on your list. Let this feeling of thankfulness fill your heart.

3. Review: At the end of the week, review your gratitude list. Notice any patterns or changes in what you're grateful for as time goes on.

Tip: Gratitude is a powerful tool for healing. By focusing on what you have, rather than what you've lost, you can begin to shift your mindset toward hope and positivity.

Exercise 3: Practicing Self-Compassion

Purpose: *To treat yourself with the kindness and understanding you would offer a friend.*

1. Acknowledge: Recognize the pain you're feeling. Say to yourself, "This is hard, but I am doing my best."

2. Encourage: Write a letter to yourself as if you were a close friend going through the same experience. Offer words of encouragement, support, and love.

3. Affirm: Create a list of affirmations that you can repeat to yourself daily. Examples might include:

- "I am strong, even when I feel weak."

- "It's okay to feel what I'm feeling."

- "I am healing, even if it's not always visible."

Tip: Keep your letter and affirmations somewhere you can easily access them. On tough days, read them aloud to remind yourself that you are deserving of kindness and compassion.

Exercise 4: Connecting with Faith

Purpose: *To strengthen your spiritual connection and find peace through prayer.*

1. Pray: Set aside a specific time each day for prayer. It could be in the morning, before bed, or whenever you feel the need to connect with God.

2. Meditate: Spend a few minutes in quiet meditation after your prayer. Focus on your breathing and allow yourself to be present in the moment. Feel God's presence surrounding you.

3. Reflect: After your prayer and meditation, write down any thoughts, feelings, or inspirations that come to you. How does your faith support you in this journey? What messages do you feel God is sending you?

Tip: If you find it difficult to pray, start with something simple, "Lord, I'm struggling today. Please help me find peace." Let your prayers be honest and from the heart.

Exercise 5: Moving Forward with Intention

Purpose: *To take proactive steps toward reclaiming your life and moving forward.*

1. Set Goals: Identify one or two small, achievable goals that will help you move forward. These could be anything from going for a daily walk, reconnecting with a hobby you love, or reaching out to a friend.

2. Take Action: Each day, take one small step toward achieving your goals. Celebrate each success, no matter how small.

3. Reflect: At the end of the week, reflect on your progress. How do you feel about the steps you've taken? What has been the most challenging? What has been the most rewarding?

Tip: Remember, progress is progress, no matter how small. Be patient with yourself and acknowledge each step forward as a victory on your path to healing.

Common grieving styles:

1. Emotional Grievers

Emotional grievers express their feelings openly and rely on talking, crying, or writing to process their grief. They are often in touch with their emotions and find comfort in sharing their experience with others.

2. Physical Grievers

Physical grievers experience grief through bodily reactions such as fatigue, headaches, or tension. They may focus on staying active or throwing themselves into physical tasks to cope with their loss.

3. Cognitive Grievers

Cognitive grievers process loss through thinking, analyzing, and reflecting. They may focus on trying to make sense of their emotions, question spiritual beliefs, or deeply contemplate the meaning of life and death.

4. Task-Oriented Grievers

Task-oriented grievers focus on action as a way to cope. They may immerse themselves in organizing events like memorial services, handling logistics, or tackling projects that keep their mind occupied.

5. Social Grievers

Social grievers seek comfort in the company of others and often cope by surrounding themselves with friends, family, or support groups. They may share stories, engage in social activities, or participate in community gatherings to ease their grief.

6. Spiritual Grievers

Spiritual grievers turn to faith, religion, or spiritual practices to help them navigate their loss. They may find comfort in prayer, meditation, scripture, or participating in spiritual rituals.

7. Avoidant Grievers

Avoidant grievers may distract themselves from the pain by staying busy or suppressing their emotions. They might avoid conversations about their loss or delay confronting their grief.

8. Creative Grievers

Creative grievers express their feelings through art, music, writing, or other forms of creative expression. They channel their emotions into something tangible, finding release and healing through their creativity.

9. Intellectual Grievers

Intellectual grievers cope by seeking information, researching grief, or reading about the experiences of others who have faced similar losses. They may focus on understanding grief from a logical perspective.

10. Silent Grievers

Silent grievers tend to keep their emotions to themselves and process their grief internally. They may not express their pain openly and could appear outwardly calm, but this doesn't mean they aren't grieving deeply.

Each grieving style is valid, and people may move between different styles over time. The most important thing is to respect how someone processes their grief and offer support in a way that honors their individual needs.

Discover Your Grieving Style – Quick Exercise

This simple exercise will help you identify how you tend to process grief. Read each statement below and rate how much you agree with it on a scale from 1 to 5.

1 = Strongly Disagree
2 = Disagree
3 = Neutral
4 = Agree
5 = Strongly Agree

Statements:

I often talk to others about my feelings when I'm grieving.

I feel grief in my body, tension or fatigue, and try to stay physically active to cope.

I spend a lot of time thinking deeply about what happened and analyzing my feelings.

When I'm grieving, I focus on practical tasks to keep myself busy.

I prefer to be around friends and family when I'm grieving.

I find comfort in spiritual practices such as prayer, meditation, or attending services.

I try to distract myself and avoid focusing too much on my grief.

I express my grief creatively, such as through writing, art, or music.

I read books or research to understand grief from a more logical perspective.

I tend to keep my feelings to myself and don't share them with others.

I find comfort by connecting with others or joining support groups when I'm grieving.

Scoring Key:

Emotional Griever: Add up your scores for **1** and **5**.

Physical Griever: Add up your score for **2**.

Cognitive Griever: Add up your score for **3**.

Task-Oriented Griever: Add up your score for **4**.

Social Griever: Add up your score for **5** and **11**.

Spiritual Griever: Add up your score for **6**.

Avoidant Griever: Add up your score for **7**.

Creative Griever: Add up your score for **8**.

Intellectual Griever: Add up your score for **9**.

Silent Griever: Add up your score for **10**.

Interpretation:

The highest score(s) represent your primary grieving style(s). If you scored similarly in multiple areas, you may process grief in a combination of ways, which is perfectly normal.

For example, if your highest scores were on statements 1 and 5, you might be an **Emotional Griever**; if you scored high on 5 and 11, you may be a **Social Griever**.

This exercise helps you gain insight into how you naturally cope with loss, allowing you to navigate grief in a way that feels authentic to you. Remember, every grieving style is valid, and you are allowed to process grief at your own pace.

Resources

National Hotline For Mental Health Crises And Suicide Prevention

800-273-TALK (8255) or 800-SUICIDE

If you or someone you know needs support, consider reaching out to a professional grief counselor, therapist, or joining a grief support group for guidance and healing.

Acknowledgements

"I am filled with gratitude as I reflect on the many people who have walked alongside me throughout the journey of writing this book. Your love, support, and encouragement have been my strength, and I couldn't have done it without you."

"To my beautiful children and grandchildren, your love and joy have been my constant inspiration. Every day, you remind me of the beauty of life and the importance of living with purpose. My greatest desire is to be an example for you—an example of strength, faith, and walking confidently in the purpose God has placed in my heart. As you continue to grow, I pray you see in me what it means to embrace your God-given purpose and live it boldly. Love you more than words can express."

To my wonderful fiancé, thank you for being my rock, encouraging me every step of the way, and believing in this dream even when I couldn't. And to my siblings, your unwavering support, love, and the bond we share have carried me through more than words can express."

To my closest friends, your presence in my life is a gift I cherish deeply. Whether it was a quick text, long conversation, or simply being there when I needed a listening ear, you all reminded me of the power of true friendship and kept me moving forward. Your encouragement has meant the world to me.

And finally, to you, my reader—thank you for choosing to walk this journey with me by picking up this book. I am truly grateful for the opportunity to share my story with you. My heartfelt hope is that these pages inspire and uplift you, and remind you that no matter where you are in life, there is always hope and light ahead.

Printed in the USA
CPSIA information can be obtained
at www.ICGtesting.com
LVHW051619211124
797039LV00019B/460
9798895892848